HAMILTON COLLEGE

RO7734AO7

D0533552

941. 34

A word about Anne and Cinde

Books are to be retur
the last date below.

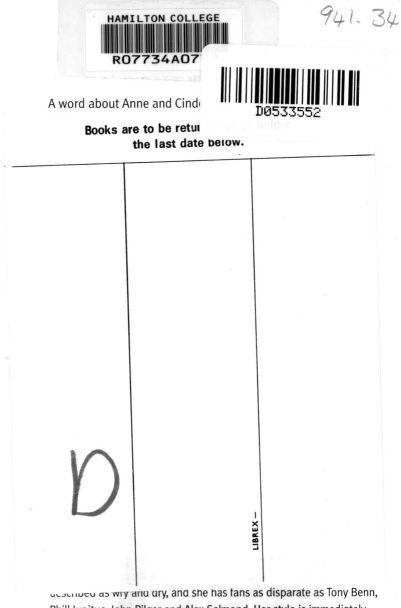

described as wry and dry, and she has fans as disparate as Tony Benn,
Phill Jupitus, John Pilger and Alex Salmond. Her style is immediately
appealing to children and young people; she brings Edinburgh's past
to life with humour and her subtlety has universal appeal.

Cinders is intrigued by the way children see the world, and her own
two constantly provide inspiration.

HAMILTON COLLEGE LIBRARY

ii

Acknowledgements
A special thanks to all who helped me with my
enquiries along the way, including: Lynn Arnott
at St Giles', Elaine Greig at The Writers'
Museum, Barb Fraser at Historic Scotland,
Patricia Brindle at Edinburgh World Heritage
Trust, and the staff at the Edinburgh Room of
the Central Library, The Outlook Tower,
Gladstone's Land, The Museum of Childhood,
John Knox House, The People's Story, Museum
of Edinburgh, Canongate Kirk, Our Dynamic
Earth and Holyrood Palace.

Let's Explore
EDINBURGH
Old Town

Anne Bruce English

Illustrations by Cinders McLeod

Luath Press Limited

EDINBURGH

www.luath.co.uk

iv

First Published 2001

The paper used in this book is acid-free, neutral-
sized and recyclable. It is made from low chlorine
pulps produced in a low energy, low emission
manner from sustainable forests.

Printed and bound by Bell & Bain Ltd., Glasgow

Designed by Tom Bee
© Luath Press Ltd

Contents

vi

Fire and Ice

The Old Town of Edinburgh began with fire and with ice. In the beginning there was a volcano. It spewed out flames and molten rock before dying. This was 340 million years ago. **Edinburgh Castle** sits on the very top of this dark rock which was once an active volcano.

Quick Quiz Where does the name volcano come from? a) the Roman god Vulcan b) the Volcanic Islands in the Pacific? *Answer on next page*

But people lived on the rock long before there was a castle. A tunnel was dug through the rock in the late 1980s. There were signs of early round houses where the castle's Cartshed restaurant is now. They may have been built about 900 BC.

A thousand years later there was a fort here. Whole families and their animals lived together. The men were ready to defend the fort.

The rock was a good place to build a fort and then a castle. The steep rock face made the castle easier to defend. Attackers had to climb the jagged rocks before reaching even the outer walls of the castle.

On the north side of the castle, where the railway line and **Princes Street Gardens** are, there was a swamp and a deep man-made loch or lake. Called the **Nor Loch** *(North Loch)*, it was full of smelly water.

The east side of the castle *(the Esplanade side)* would always be the easiest to attack. The castle entrance was built here. It has been altered many times and had a dry ditch, a drawbridge, outer and inner doors and a portcullis for defence at different times.

Long before this, after the heat and fire of the volcano had died, came the ice. The slow-moving sheets of ice wore away the softer rock and carried it downhill. It built up as a high ridge with steep sides. So the castle is on the top of the volcano and the first houses were built on the high ridge – the beginning of the **Old Town** of Edinburgh.

Quick Quiz answer
a) From Vulcan, the Roman god of fire.

The Old Town

The first houses were built near the castle with long sloping gardens behind them. So many people wanted to live in Edinburgh that houses were soon built on the gardens. They were reached by narrow lanes between the older houses.

Then disaster struck the Scottish nation. On 9th September 1513 the Scots were defeated by the troops of King Henry VIII at the Battle of Flodden, just across the border into England. The Scottish king, James IV, was one of those killed on the battlefield. Thousands of Scots died.

This battle had an effect on Edinburgh for hundreds of years. Afraid that Edinburgh would be attacked next, the townspeople began to build a new and stronger wall to protect their town.

They must have run out of time, energy or money because it was 47 years before the **Flodden Wall** was finished. It enclosed three sides of the town and the Nor Loch protected the fourth side. You can see parts of the Flodden Wall in the Old Town today – in **Greyfriars Churchyard** and at the foot of **St Mary's Street**.

The last building on the **High Street**, just inside the Flodden Wall, was called **World's End**.

For the frightened people it was the end of their safe world. The name has never been changed.

Because everyone wanted to live inside the wall, the only way to build was up, higher and higher. The Old Town became a very smelly town.

Danger Gardyloo!

This one word, Gardyloo, warned of danger overhead. It came every day. Windows were opened and with a single cry 'Gardyloo' *(from the French 'Beware of the water')* all the household rubbish and slops were emptied out into the street.

Local people took cover but there are stories of visitors looking up when they heard the cry – and getting drenched. It's best not to ask what was in the hundreds of pails and pots being emptied.

None of the tall buildings in the Old Town had plumbing or drains. Diseases spread quickly. Cholera was spread through infected water. A tiny bite from a rat flea could give you deadly plague – and the rats fed on the rubbish lying in the street.

Each of the tall buildings had one stair, shared by everyone who lived there.

Noblemen and merchants, shoemakers, shopkeepers and labourers would all live in the same building. The middle floors were the best, away from the noise and smells of the street and with not too many stairs to climb.

Although the houses had no water they had chimneys and fireplaces. The smoke from hundreds of coal fires hung over the town, blotting out the sunlight. Edinburgh earned the nickname 'Auld Reekie' *(Old Smoky)*.

When the first houses were built in the **New Town** in the late 18th century, the richer people moved there. The poorer people stayed in the Old Town. The grand rooms were divided into smaller and smaller rooms and more people moved in. They even lived in the cellars, with no daylight or fresh air. If there was a corner to spare, it was rented to a lodger.

Life was like this for a very long time. What did change was that the long main street of the Old Town was given a new name – **The Royal Mile.**

The Royal Mile

From Edinburgh Castle on its high rock down to the **Palace of Holyroodhouse** is now known as **The Royal Mile.**

Royal Mile Fact File

1. *It's called royal because the castle and the Palace of Holyroodhouse have been royal residences.*
2. *The royal family still stay at Holyrood on official visits to Edinburgh.*

3. From the castle to Holyrood measures a little over one mile.
4. The tall buildings are 'lands' or tenements.
5. The narrow passageway between the tall buildings is a close or a wynd.
6. Some of the closes open out into a wider court with buildings all round it.

Names in the Royal Mile

Most of the tenements and closes have had more than one name. It could be the name of the person who built it or just someone who lived there. Other names tell you what work was done there. The names are above the entrance to the close or carved on the pavement.

In the **Lawnmarket** there's **Gladstone's Land,** called after wealthy Thomas Gladstone, and **Wardrop's Court** named after John Wardrop, a carpenter. A fountain or well stood outside **Fountain Close** in the High Street and **Anchor Close** was the home of the Anchor Tavern.

Below **St Giles'** Cathedral is **Old Fishmarket**

Close, where there was a fish market. Local people complained of the smell as fish was thrown on to the street and left there.

Opposite St Giles is the name of a close which no longer exists. **Old Post Office Close** was closed in 1932. For a time it was Edinburgh's only Post Office, with one postman to deliver letters to all of the Old Town.

The 21st Century

The days of 'Gardyloo' are gone. The days of overcrowded tenements are gone. But people still live, and come to work, in the Old Town. And the Old Town goes on changing.

Look for:-

NEW BUILDINGS

The **Scandic Crowne Plaza,** a hotel on the corner of High Street and **Niddry Street**. It looks like a huge Scottish castle.

The **Scottish Poetry Library, Crichton's Court,** off the **Canongate**. It won a Civic Trust Award in 2000 for its design – low and modern but with an outside stair. Open to the public.

Dynamic Earth, on Holyrood Road, also won a Civic Trust Award in 2000. It has a curving front, and a domed top like a billowing sail.

THE SCOTTISH PARLIAMENT

It was elected in 1999 and meets in the Old Town. The new Parliament is being built close to **Holyrood,** at the foot of the Royal Mile. Until it's ready, Parliament meets in the **Assembly Hall of the Church of Scotland.** There are entrances from the Lawnmarket. Parliamentary signs in blue are written in English and Gaelic.

Before the Assembly Hall was built, the mother of Mary Queen of Scots had a palace on the same site.

THE CLOSES OF THE OLD TOWN

Some of the closes still have locked gates and
there's no entry. Many more have been
restored. You can walk through some of them.
They're what Edinburgh calls 'pedestrian-
friendly' routes, a short cut from one part of the
town to another.

Advocate's Close runs from the top of the
High Street to the foot of Cockburn Street.
It takes you to Waverley Station and coach
tours starting on Waverley Bridge. There are
reminders of the long-distant past in the close.
Two old doorways are dated 1590, and have
initials and mottoes carved in the stone.

Chalmer's Close, in the lower half of the
High Street, cuts down to Jeffrey Street and The
City Arts Centre and Fruitmarket Gallery.
On the way is the Brass Rubbing Centre
(open during the summer months).

FESTIVAL TIME

Flags, banners and streamers decorate the
streets. There are so many people that the High
Street near St Giles' is closed to traffic. Stalls
are set up in the street and musicians, jugglers,
stilt-walkers and fire-eaters entertain. The
Festival Fringe Society is at 180 High Street.
It has an eye-catching frontage. Look for bright
blue paint and green and red diamond-
patterned legs.

The spectacular Military Tattoo takes place
on the castle esplanade. For the once-a-year
Firework Concert, the fireworks are set off from
the castle rock. You can see some of the display
from the Old Town but the view is better from
the New Town.

LIVING IN THE OLD TOWN TODAY

This is now much more pleasant. Flats for sale or to let are popular, but there are problems. The main ones are traffic, noise *(although it's much quieter in the closes and courts than on the main road),* and shopping. Visitors can buy postcards, souvenirs and Scottish knitwear from **Castlehill** to the gates of Holyrood. There are fewer shops for daily essentials like food, chemist's goods, Post Office and Banks.

Castle and Esplanade

Quick Quiz   If someone gave you a piece of Edinburgh Rock would you a) eat it or b) keep it as a souvenir? *Answer on next page*

The Castle *(in the care of Historic Scotland),* has over 1 million visitors a year and is Scotland's top paid tourist attraction. You need a ticket to visit the castle. Look for the tiny **St Margaret's Chapel,** and for the **Honours of**

Scotland in the Crown Room. Lying beside the crown, sword and sceptre is the Stone of Destiny. It was returned to Scotland in 1996.

There's also a new exhibition on the famous **One O'clock Gun**. Remember, if you're visiting at one o'clock, the gun is fired *(not Sundays)*.

The two statues on the castle gatehouse are **King Robert the Bruce** *(on the left)* and **Sir William Wallace** *(on the right)*. Mel Gibson's £80 million film, *Braveheart,* was about the life and times of William Wallace.

The Esplanade is the open area in front of the castle. It was a 19th century parade ground for soldiers living in the castle. The statues and memorials around the Esplanade are military ones. They're hidden during the annual **Edinburgh Festival** by seating for the Military Tattoo. This is a colourful and noisy event, although it can be chilly, even on an August evening, sitting high up in the open air.

One memorial, at the foot of the Esplanade, tells a sad story. It's the **Witches' Well,** put there in memory of 300 women who were accused of being witches and then killed close to this spot.

On a clear day there are good views from here to the north, across the River Forth to the Kingdom of Fife. All this is hidden when the well-known 'haar', a cold damp mist, rolls in from the sea.

Quick Quiz answer a) eat it. Edinburgh Rock is a soft sweet candy, made in short ribbed sticks and flavoured.

Castlehill and Lawnmarket

Quick Quiz 1 Look at the first building on **Castlehill,** going downhill. It's a plain one-storey building, built in 1849 to store something. Do you think it was for a) coal or b) water, for the houses in the Old Town.
Answer on page 12

Castlehill starts just outside the Esplanade. It's narrow and steep. If you're exploring the Old Town on foot, then walking from the castle to Holyrood is all downhill.

Quick Quiz 2 The Quick Quiz 1 building is now the Tartan Weaving Mill and Exhibition. Among the tartans is an Edinburgh tartan in bright colours of blue, red, green and white. Does it date from 1950, 1970 or 1990?
Answer on page 12

Next to the Quick Quiz building is the **Outlook Tower** and **Camera Obscura.** There are 100 steps to the top. It's not a film the Camera Obscura shows you but a view of what is happening outside. You can count the endless stream of buses travelling along Princes Street, see the colour of people's clothes, watch them looking in shop windows and waiting to cross the streets. The clearer the day, the further you can see.

At the foot of Castlehill is a building with the tallest spire in Edinburgh. It was the **Highland Tolbooth Church,** built 1839–44. In 1999 it became **The Hub,** the **Edinburgh Festival Centre,** with information, tickets, food and a shop inside.

Across the road from The Hub is a wall sign for a narrow cobbled street, the **Upper Bow.** It leads to **Victoria Terrace** where there's a map and information on the very old **West Bow.** It was one of the earliest Edinburgh streets. Below you is **Victoria Street,** built in 1840 and linking **George IV Bridge** and the **Grassmarket.**

The **Lawnmarket** *(Landmarket)* would have been one of the busiest places in the Old Town, and one of the noisiest. On Wednesday cloth was sold there. On other days milk, butter, cheese and vegetables were brought in from the country. Stalls were set up in the street. Pedlars carried goods to sell or pushed handcarts. They all called out their wares and the prices. Shoppers wandered around, comparing prices before buying.

At the top of the Lawnmarket, outside The Hub, a traffic roundabout is painted on the road. The Old Weigh House stood here. On market days butter and cheese were weighed out there.

There have always been traffic problems in the Old Town. The Weigh House was knocked down to widen the road in 1822 before a visit from King George IV.

Quick Quiz 1 answer b) water. It was a resevoir, replacing one built as long ago as 1681.

Quick Quiz 2 answer Edinburgh tartan dates from 1970. It was used for the Commonwealth Games held in Edinburgh that year.

LEFT, DOWNHILL SIDE OF THE LAWNMARKET

Birds, books and beasts can all be found here. There are hanging signs for two of them, the last one you must hunt for.

Birds. The gilded bird is made of steel and copper. It hangs above the entrance to **Gladstone's Land,** wings outstretched and its prey held in its claws. The bird is a Gled, a Scottish name for a Kite, one of the Falcon family. The wealthy Thomas Gledstanes remodelled this 6 storey Land between 1617 and 1620.

It's a rare survivor of an Old Town tenement, with the arched entrance and a narrow outside stair. A sleeping pig lies in a box outside the door. More about pigs in *'Old Town Tales: Pig Tales.' (Restored. National Trust for Scotland. Usually open April to October.)*

Books. The books are part of the sign outside **Lady Stair's Close.** The sign shows a writer at his desk, using a quill pen. The same sign hangs inside the Close on **The Writers' Museum.**

THE WRITERS' MUSEUM

This was Lady Stair's house. She owned it from 1719 but it's much older than that. Carved above the door is a date, initials and a religious motto. *1622 WG : GS – Fear the Lord and Depart from Evil*

The house was built in 1622 for William Gray and his wife Geida Smith. In the museum are more books, papers and letters, portraits, walking sticks and riding boots belonging to three Scottish writers, **Robert Burns, Sir Walter Scott** and **Robert Louis Stevenson.** You can even see examples of their handwriting. Burns' is round

and bold, Stevenson's is much more spikey, while Scott's is a flowing scrawl, as if he was always in a hurry. All three have connections with the Old Town.
See 'People of the Old Town'

Makars' Court is a new name in the Lawnmarket. The close outside the Writers' Museum has quotations from Scottish writers set in the paving. More will be added over the years.

Beasts. The four fierce beasts are harder to find. They have scaly bodies, long tails, wings, curved teeth and claws. They're dragons and they guard **Wardrop's Court,** two at the entrance and two through the archway.

RIGHT, DOWNHILL SIDE OF THE LAWNMARKET

People. Three important people lived here. One was a rogue, another was a philosopher and the third was murdered.

OLD TOWN TALES:
A Double Life

Deacon William Brodie was a rogue. He lived and worked in **Brodie's Close.** By day he was a hard-working man, a wright or joiner, and an official or Deacon of his trade.

Because of his work he visited many of the Old Town shops. The shopkeepers often kept the shop keys hanging on the back of the door. William Brodie secretly took wax impressions of the keys, then had copies made.

At night he used the copied keys to rob his friends, selling what he stole to pay his debts. No-one suspected the busy Deacon of being a thief.

But one night Brodie and his gang were disturbed while robbing the Excise Office in the Canongate. Brodie fled to Amsterdam. Two hundred pounds was offered for his capture, a huge sum in 1788. He was captured in Amsterdam, hiding in a cupboard.

Brodie was brought back to Edinburgh, tried in court and sentenced to hang. On the 1st October 1788 he went to the gallows outside St. Giles' cathedral, smartly dressed in a good black suit. Earlier he had been asked by the Town Council to improve the gallows. He was the first person to use it.

Robert Louis Stevenson may have based his famous story, The Strange Case of Dr. Jekyll and Mr. Hyde, on William Brodie and his double life of good and evil. There's another strange connection between the two men. As a child Stevenson had a cabinet in his room which was made by Brodie. It's now in the Stevenson room of the Writers' Museum.

David Hume was a philosopher and historian. At one time his family home was in **Riddles Court**. In 1997 a statue of him was put up outside the High Court, at the top of **Bank Street**. He sits, with bare feet and very few clothes, on one of Edinburgh's many windy corners.

Bailie John Macmorran was an important man. He was a Town Councillor, a magistrate and very wealthy. He lived in Riddles Court. This is how he met a sad end.

OLD TOWN TALES: Boys Behaving (very) Badly

In September 1595 there was a riot at Edinburgh's High School. The schoolboys had asked for extra holidays but had been refused them. They locked themselves in the building. From somewhere they produced hidden weapons. This was so serious that Bailie John Macmorran was sent for.

He tried to reason with the boys. They refused to listen, shouting threats to him through the locked door. 'Batter down the door,' ordered the Bailie. Those were his last words. From a window a single shot rang out. Bailie John Macmorran dropped dead, a bullet through his head.

The terrified boys unlocked the door. They named the guilty boy as William Sinclair, son of Lord Sinclair of Caithness. A few of the boys were locked in the **Tolbooth Jail,** but then set free. William Sinclair was never brought to trial.

The Sinclair family did make an apology to the Macmorran family, but nothing more. The Town Council and the Macmorrans were most unhappy with this. Even the King refused to help them and there was nothing more they could do.

The Grassmarket, Greyfriars Church and Churchyard
– not forgetting Bobby.

This is all part of the Old Town but not part of the Royal Mile.

Quick Quiz Was Greyfriars Bobby
a) a policeman (nicknamed a 'bobby') or
b) a dog? *Answer on page 22*

Many years ago an open air market was held in the **Grassmarket. Greyfriars** did have Grey Friars, members of the Franciscan religious order who wore grey. Over hundreds of years the names have not been changed.

Many horrible events happened in this part of the Old Town, but it did see some happier times. All Hallows Fair, held in the Grassmarket on 1st November each year, was noisy, lively and colourful. There was plenty to eat and drink, magicians and jugglers entertained in the street and strolling players set up a small stage and acted for their audience.

The West Bow, that old, steep and zigzag road from the Grassmarket to Castlehill, saw kings and queens riding to the castle or to the Palace at Holyrood. They were welcomed to Edinburgh with music, poetry and speeches. The silver keys of the town were presented to them, as they still are today.

THE KEYS OF THE CITY

The earliest keys, which were handed to Mary
Queen of Scots, have been lost. The keys used
today were first given to King Charles I in 1633.
They're made of Scottish silver and are about
20 centimetres long. The two keys are crossed,
tied with black and white ribbon *(the colours of
the city)* and laid on a red velvet cushion. The
cushion is edged with gold braid. The keys are
presented to the Sovereign and then handed
back to the city for safekeeping.

But between 1661 and 1688 the
Grassmarket was known for a more gruesome
reason. It was a place of public execution,
mainly of Covenanters. The final years are
remembered as 'The Killing Times'.

The Covenanters.

*The Covenanters wanted to worship in
the Scottish way, without using the new
English prayer book or having bishops.
Many of them signed the National
Covenant in 1638 to keep their own form
of worship. The worst times for the
Covenanters were when King Charles II
returned to the throne in 1660. He was
followed by his brother, King James II,
who died in 1688. These were the years
of arrests and transportation. Many died
for their faith.*

The scaffold stood near the foot of Victoria
Street. Close by is the **Covenanters' Memorial.**
On the low stone wall round it is a list of
100 men and 2 women who were executed
in Edinburgh.

The list starts on 27th May 1661 with the Marquis of Argyll and ends on 17th February 1688 with James Renwick, 'minister on the moors'. Many ministers of the Church of Scotland had been put out of their churches. James Renwick held secret open-air services in the Braid Hills. He must have been discovered or betrayed.

TWO POETS AND FOUR ROADS

Two poets. The Grassmarket is lined with places to eat, from new coffee shops to old pubs. One of the oldest is the White Hart Inn. The poet Robert Burns stayed there on his last visit to Edinburgh (1791). The English poet William Wordsworth and his sister Dorothy also stayed there, in 1803. Dorothy wrote in her journal that the inn was *'not noisy and tolerably cheap.'*

Four roads. The Grassmarket is long and wide, with an old road at each corner. The four names tell you about their past.

1. **King's Stables Road,** at the foot of the castle rock, where horses were stabled. Now there are only cars in a multi-storey car park.

2. **West Port,** the gateway into the walled town from the west.

3. **Cowgate,** once a country lane where cattle were led out to graze.

4. **Candlemaker Row,** the hill where the candlemakers worked. Local people avoided the Row. They were afraid of fire and hated the smell of melting wax. It was often tallow, an animal fat, which smells foul.

GREYFRIARS

At the top of **Candlemaker Row** is Greyfriars, the church on the right and the statue of **Greyfriars Bobby** on the left. Just inside the church gates is a memorial stone to Bobby. Sometimes there are flowers laid beside it.

Bobby's master, John Gray *(Auld Jock),* is also buried in Greyfriars. The new red granite headstone was put there by American lovers of Bobby. A Walt Disney film about Bobby's life means his story is known all over the world.

The shadow of the Covenanters lies over the church and the churchyard. The National Covenant was signed in the church. Much later, hundreds of Covenanter prisoners were held in an open prison in what is now part of the churchyard. Many died from cold and hunger.

A length of the Flodden Wall runs through the churchyard, behind the church. Some of the headstones in the churchyard are very old. They have worn carvings of skeletons, skulls and crossed bones, like those on pirate flags. Other tombs have metal bars laid over a flat tombstone. They're reminders of another infamous time in Edinburgh's past – the time of the Body Snatchers. They searched for the bodies of the newly buried to sell to the medical school. The students learned about the human body by studying the corpse. In the 1820s there was a large increase in students and the number of classes, and so more bodies were needed.

OLD TOWN TALES:
The Story of Burke and Hare –
Murder and Money

Burke and Hare were not body snatchers. They found another way to get bodies, and to get paid for them. The pair lived in the West Port. When an old man died in their lodgings, Hare claimed he was owed money. He decided to sell the body. Burke agreed.

Together they took the body to Dr. Robert Knox at the medical school, and were paid £7.10s (£7.50). They were in business.

At the beginning they were very careful, choosing victims who were strangers to the Grassmarket. They smothered them in their lodgings and then sold the bodies to Dr. Knox. He asked no questions, even when the pair had sold him 16 or so bodies.

Then Burke and Hare became greedy. They killed a local girl. Some of the medical students recognised her. They knew she had been in good health. Then Daft Jamie, a harmless but well-known local lad, was killed.

Then a body was discovered hidden in the West Port house. The police were called and Burke and Hare were arrested. Hare put all the blame on Burke and gave evidence against him in court.

Burke was found guilty and hanged. Hare went free. But an angry mob were after him and he had to flee Edinburgh. Dr. Knox found that fewer students came to his lectures and he was never offered promotion.

Although all this happened nearly 200 years ago, the names of William Burke and William Hare are still remembered in the stories of Edinburgh's past.

HAMILTON COLLEGE

Quick Quiz answer b) a dog. Greyfriars Bobby was a Skye terrier. When his master, John Gray died, Bobby sat faithfully by his grave for 14 years. There's a statue of Bobby near Greyfriars church. Many visitors have a photograph taken beside it.

High Street 1

LAWNMARKET TO NORTH AND SOUTH BRIDGES

Quick Quiz In this part of the Old Town there's an **Old Assembly Close** and a **New Assembly Close.** What kind of Assembly met there a) a Town Council Assembly b) a Dancing Assembly. *Answer on page 27*

This part of the High Street is built on the very top of the Old Town ridge. The closes and wynds slope very steeply downhill, away from the street. On the north *(downhill left)* side, Advocate's Close is long and steep, a mix of steps and slopes. Even walking a short way down the close and looking back, you can imagine how many people must have lived in one small part of the High Street.

NEW ASSEMBLY CLOSE

Old Fishmarket Close, below St. Giles' Cathedral, is also very steep. It's a surprise to see cars driving down the close towards the Cowgate. The wide arched entrance is decorated with a line of swimming fish.

Six of the most important buildings in the High Street were crowded together around St Giles'.

THE BIG SIX

1. **St Giles' Cathedral,** at one time the only church in the Old Town.
2. **Parliament Hall,** in **Parliament Square**, was used by the Scottish parliament until the 1707 Act of Union. Then the Scottish and English parliaments were united, meeting in London. In 1999, a Scottish parliament was elected again, meeting in the Old Town.
3. **The Law Courts** were also in Parliament Square. The writer Sir Walter Scott practised here.
4. **Tolbooth,** which ended its life as a dreaded prison.
5. **Old Mercat** *(Market)* Cross, a place for meetings and entertainment.
6. **The Royal Exchange,** now the City Chambers.

How many have survived?

Five of the Big Six have survived. Only the Tollbooth has been pulled down (1817). It stood very close to the west door of St Giles. A heart-shaped design set in the cobble stones, and brass plates on the roadway, mark the outline of the building.

It was a gloomy, dingy and depressing place. One man who visited the prison said he could smell it before he reached it, *'not only the smell of poor drains but the smell of human misery.'*

The Mercat Cross has survived, although only a small part of it is old. Official announcements of coronations or the Dissolution of Parliament are made from the Mercat Cross.

ST GILES' TODAY

Six things to see in St Giles' *(numbered on the plan)*

1. **Oldest** Four of the great pillars in the nave are 600 to 700 years old. They survived when the church was set on fire in 1385.
2. **Newest** The church organ is one of the newest additions (1992). The case is of Austrian oak stained a deep red. The colour translates as 'Scots Blood'.
3. **Biggest** The Thistle Chapel was added in 1911. It's the home of the Knights of the Thistle, a Scottish order of chivalry.

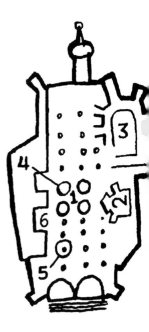

> *The Thistle Chapel was built using Scottish materials. The floor is Ailsa Craig granite inset with Iona marble. The wood is Scottish oak and the stone is from Fife. On the back of the heavy wooden doors are thistle-shaped door knobs. Look above the door for a carved wooden angel with puffed out cheeks, playing bagpipes.*

4. **Smallest** The stone masons who helped to build St Giles' carved their marks on some of the stones. Each mark is different. It's like a signature, saying 'I worked here.'
5. **Best known** On the outside, the crown steeple with a golden weathercock on top. Inside, the statue of John Knox, minister of St Giles' from 1559 to 1572. It's by the grandly named Pittendrigh MacGillivray.
6. **Least known** When St Giles' was the only public building in Edinburgh, it was used as a

place of business. St Eloi's Aisle was where the Hammermen met *(craftsmen who worked in metal)*. They would show examples of their work to customers, walk up and down the church together discussing styles and prices, then seal the business deal by striking a hand on the altar.

Edinburgh District Court and the legal profession are still in Parliament Square, behind St. Giles'. From Monday to Friday the church and the law meet daily in the Lower Aisle Restaurant in St. Giles'. Dark suited figures cross Parliament Square for coffee or a light lunch. They arrive together, sit together, (usually in the smoking area), eat together, and go on talking.

Opposite St Giles' is the **City Chambers,** the headquarters of the City of Edinburgh Council. Everything from Council Tax and Transport to Dog Wardens and Wheelie Bins is organised through them.

In the open courtyard is the unnamed door to **Mary King's Close,** known as the most haunted part of Edinburgh. *See 'Ghost Tales of the Old Town'.* Beside it a plaque tells us of the last night Mary Queen of Scots spent in Edinburgh.

OLD TOWN TALES: Taxi!

Downhill from the City Chambers is **Old Stamp Office Close.** This was the home of the tall and stately Countess of Eglinton. Like a fairy story, she had seven beautiful daughters. The family had also lived at **Jack's Land** in the Canongate. From there they travelled uphill to the dancing assemblies in the High Street.

Dressed in fine gowns and feathers, with thin-soled dancing slippers, the ladies had no intention of walking to the dance. Instead they used the taxi of the time – the sedan chair.

A chair took one person, so the Countess and her daughters formed a procession. Eight chairs paraded up the High Street. People stopped to watch these elegant ladies pass by.

Some wealthy people had private chairs but most people hired an ordinary black sedan chair. There's one in **Museum of Edinburgh** in the Canongate.

Like a taxi, you could call for a chair at any time, although it cost more after midnight. Like a taxi, a chair was hired from an official stance or waiting place. There was a set 'table of fares'. Members of the Society of Chairmen *(carriers of the chairs)* had their own badge.

The chair was like a tall upright box, with a door and windows. The seat was more like a narrow shelf. A wooden pole slotted through either side of the chair. Two chairmen carried the poles, one at the front and one behind.

The sedan chair was ideal for Edinburgh's narrow alleys and closes. But the steep streets and any overweight passengers would make carrying a difficult task for the chairmen.

One eccentric judge walked to his home in the Canongate in all weathers. Only if it was very wet did he hire a sedan chair – and then he sent his wig home in it. He walked and got wet.

THE TRON KIRK
(Christ's Kirk at the Tron)

The main waiting place for sedan chairs was close to the **Tron Kirk,** on the corner of the High Street and **South Bridge**. A Tron was a public weighing machine. This one weighed salt. Part of the Tron Kirk was pulled down when South Bridge was built. The Kirk is open for the summer as the **Old Town Information Centre**. Inside the Tron Kirk excavations have uncovered **Marlin's Wynd,** a cobbled street more than 400 years old, running down to the Cowgate.

Quick Quiz answer b) a dancing assembly. The weekly dance was a highlight of 18th century life in the Old Town.

The Great Fire of 1842

THE EDINBURGH READERS NEWS
18TH NOVEMBER 1842

The Old Town of Edinburgh is beginning to recover from the greatest fire it has ever known.

The fire started in Old Assembly Close. At ten o'clock at night smoke was seen pouring from a second floor window. Fire engines and their crews were soon on the scene, as were soldiers from the castle.

Unhappily, the entry to the close is so narrow that the fire crews could not get near to the source of the fire. The flames began to spread. Soon three tenements were ablaze.

Flames and sparks rose high into the air, while red hot embers were thrown into the night sky. Watchers covered their faces against the choking smoke.

Worse was to follow. The night had been still but then a strong wind arose, fanning the flames. Back tenements as far as the Cowgate began blazing, with flames shooting from the chimneypots.

The firemen and soldiers worked on without rest. By morning the fire seemed to be out. The weary residents of the High Street felt they could return to homes which were undamaged.

But they were not safe yet. Sparks from the fire are believed to have smouldered in the wooden steeple of the Tron Kirk. It was now seen to be ablaze.

Crowds watched in silence as the spire of their local kirk was consumed by flames. "It's a judgement upon us all," was one comment overheard, a reference to the dancing assemblies once held in the close.

By the evening of Tuesday 16th, all was quiet. But again, and at ten o'clock at night, the fire was seen to have spread. Part of Parliament Square was now blazing. Even St Giles seemed to be in danger as flames lit up the sky around it. Fortunately the great church was spared.

At last, after 50 hours, the fire was out. Many buildings have collapsed. Others are left as heaps of charred rubble and wood. Because of overcrowding in the lands and closes of the High Street it is not known how many have lost their lives. Expert opinion puts it at not more than ten.

Four hundred families are homeless. Only a few have rescued furniture. For the others, everything has been destroyed. Women and children are seen weeping openly in the street.

Edinburgh has a bad record for fires. Much of the Old Town from St Giles' to the Tron Kirk now needs rebuilding. Mr James Braidwood, director of fire engines, believes that drastic action must be taken. It is promised that this will start soon.

Postscript 1. The wooden steeple of the Tron Kirk was replaced by a stone spire in 1828.

Postscript 2. James Braidwood was made Master of Fire Engines in Edinburgh. He founded the first town fire service in the whole country. Later, he moved to the City of London where he was killed in 1861 while fighting a fire.

Five, Four, Three, Two, One

*5 statues, 4 wells, 3 shops, 2 volcanoes and
1 'Year 2000' success story*

FIVE STATUES AND PLAQUES

(all these are in the High Street)

1. The statue in Parliament Square is of **King Charles II** on horseback. It's a very early statue made of lead (1685). It's so heavy that the horse became bandy-legged. The statue has often needed repair. At one time it was even painted white. After the Great Fire of 1824 it spent 9 years stored in Calton Jail.

2. The very tall statue outside St Giles' is of the **5th Duke of Buccleuch.**

3. In the courtyard of the City Chambers is a lively bronze statue of the **Emperor Alexander** *(Alexander the Great)* and his horse **Bucephalus.**

4. The plaque on the wall of 231 High Street is of **James Gillespie.** With his brother, John, he made and sold snuff. The plaque shows James with a large nose, a jutting chin and what looks like a nightcap on his head.

5. 219 High Street – the circular plaque at first floor level is a rare memorial to a woman. **Elsie Inglis** was one of the first women to study medicine at Edinburgh University. She set up a surgery for poor women and their children at this address.

FORMERLY
THE SHOP OF
JAMES GILLESPIE
OF SPYLAW
TOBACCO AND SNUFF
MANUFACTURER
FOUNDER OF
JAMES GILLESPIE'S
HOSPITAL
AND SCHOOLS
DIED 8 APRIL 1797

ERECTED BY
THE GOVERNOR 1838

FOUR WELLS OR WELLHEADS

Four of the Old Town wells or wellheads are still in place and easy to find.

1. In the Grassmarket, the West Bow Well of 1674 is at the foot of Victoria Street. The traffic has to drive round it.

2, 3 and **4.** These 3 wells stand on the pavements of the High Street. There's a large well close to George IV Bridge *(opposite the statue of David Hume).* Lower down, outside Old Assembly Close, the High Street Wellhead is smaller. It dates from around 1675 and was renewed in 1997. The water spouts are faces with open mouths. The renewed Netherbow Wellhead is outside **Moubray House** and is a larger one.

The Old Town tenements of 6, 7 or 8 storeys had no water at all. Water Caddies earned a living by carrying water to the different households in the tall tenements.

THREE SHOPS
(all with links to the past. Can you find them?)

1. The Bagpipe shop in **James Court,** off the Lawnmarket, is one of the few left in the Old Town. The bagpipe makers work in an old arched stone cellar under the Lawnmarket.

2. The Cigar shop opposite St Giles has a very old shop sign standing at the door. It's a carved figure of an American Indian with cigars tucked into his belt. These shop signs were used when many people could not read.

3. Lower down the High Street, the name
Luckenbooth is a reminder of the locked
booths or shops which crowded round
St Giles'. By 1817 the road was barely
wide enough for a horse and cart to pass.
The Luckenbooths were knocked down.

TWO VOLCANOES

1. Edinburgh Castle is built on an
extinct volcano.

2. At the bottom of the Royal Mile there's
another. It's in **Holyrood Park** and is called
Arthur's Seat. At 251 metres it's the highest
of Edinburgh's hills.

ONE 'YEAR 2000' SUCCESS STORY

Our Dynamic Earth is on Holyrood Road, near
the Palace. It cost £34 million to build. £15m
of that came from the Millennium Commission.
It tells the story of our planet. You can feel part
of an earthquake, an active volcano, a polar
landscape and a tropical rainstorm *(but you
don't get wet)*.

High Street 2

*NORTH & SOUTH BRIDGES TO JEFFREY STREET
& ST MARY'S STREET*

Quick Quiz 1 Some families in the High Street
kept a pig. Did the pig live a) in the back garden
b) under the stairs? *Answer on page* 38

Looking down the High Street from the Bridges
junction you see a long, straight and wide
street. It's only at the very foot that the road
narrows. This is where the old **Netherbow Port**
or **Gate** stood. It guarded the most important

entrance to the Old Town of Edinburgh. Most of the interesting buildings are in this part of the street.

LEFT, DOWNHILL SIDE OF THE HIGH STREET

Paisley Close, which is nearer the North Bridge, has its own dramatic story to tell.

OLD TOWN TALES: A Crash in the Night

Carved above the entrance to Paisley Close is the head of a pleasant-faced young man. The words above his head read, *'Heave Awa' Chaps, I'm No Dead Yet.'*

They're a reminder of an Old Town disaster. In the early hours of 24th November 1861 this whole tenement collapsed. All the floors, from top to bottom, crashed down, filling the street with rubble and choking dust. The young man who survived was Joseph McIvor.

There had been signs that the building was unsafe. Doors kept sticking and there was a bulge in one wall. None of the seven landlords came to look at the building.

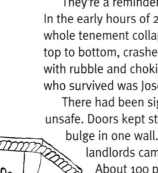

About 100 people were sleeping there when it collapsed. Thirty five were killed. Many more were badly hurt. James McIvor was one of those buried in the rubble. He must have heard the rescuers digging for survivors. That was when he called out, 'Heave awa' chaps, I'm no' dead yet.' His voice was heard and he was saved.

When the tenement was rebuilt the carving was put up as a reminder of what happened that night.

34

Postscript Some good came out of this disaster. In 1862, 35 year old Dr. Henry Duncan Littlejohn became the first Medical Officer for Health for Edinburgh *(and the first in Scotland)*. He spent a lifetime working to improve the living conditions for the people of the Old Town.

Much nearer the foot of the High Street are two of Edinburgh's oldest buildings. One is Moubray House, first built for a Robert Moubray in the late 15th century. The house is tall and narrow, like Gladstone's Land in the Lawnmarket. If you walk into **Trunk's Close,** down the side of Moubray House, you'll find a new but hidden garden. It's an oasis of green among the old and new stone buildings.

Like Gladstone's Land, Moubray House still has an outside stair leading to the first floor. Over many years the steps had become worn and dangerous and have been renewed.

OLD TOWN TALES: Pig tales

Edinburgh people complained that outside stairs were a nuisance. They took up too much space on the busy street. But the nuisance was worse than that.

Some households kept pigs under the outside stair. There was a low door under the stair and a pigsty inside. The pigs spent the summer days roaming through the High Street, searching the rubbish dumps for scraps to eat.

In the winter they were killed and salted
for food.

While the pigs wandered around freely in
the daytime, at night they were called back
home and shut in the pigsties again. Of course
not all of them did go home. For more than 300
years there were complaints about the menace
of Edinburgh's wandering pigs.

There were even notices in newspapers
about pigs, lost and found. This is one from 1st
August 1754. *'If any person has lost a large sow
let them call at the house of Robert Fiddes...
upon proving the pig is theirs, and paying
expenses and damages done by the sow, they
can have it back.'*

Robert Fiddes was a gardener so the pig
may have ruined his garden.

Not everyone disliked the pigs. Two well
brought up little girls had their morning fun
riding up and down the High Street on the back
of a large and friendly pig. The eccentric Lord
Gardenstone let his pet pig sleep in his bed.
When it grew too big, it slept on the floor on
top of his clothes. He said it warmed them up
for the next morning. No-one seemed bothered
by the smell.

Whenever there were royal visits or
processions the pigs were kept off the street.
The rubbish tips were cleared away. The
outside stair was cleaned and hung with
carpets and tapestries. As soon as the special
occasion was over the pigs were back again.

JOHN KNOX HOUSE
– a House of Secrets

Close to Moubray House is this house, the second of the two old houses in this part of the High Street. This is where the street narrows. The house must be one of the best known in Edinburgh. It has a red tiled roof, tall chimneys, and a gallery, like an enclosed balcony, on the first floor.

The secret it keeps hidden is this – did the Scots preacher, John Knox, live here at all? If he did it was only at the very end of his life. He died in the house in 1572 and the room has a stained glass window with a portrait of him, a thin hand stroking his long beard.

Because the house has his name it's been saved from demolition. There were suggestions that it should be pulled down to widen this part of the street.

So who did live in John Knox's house? The answer is on the wall. His name was James Mossman, and he was a jeweller and goldsmith. He made the crown you can see in Ediburgh Castle's Crown Room.

- The initials on the outside wall are I(J) M, and MA for James Mossman's wife, Mariota Arres.

- Mossman made jewellery and lent money to Mary Queen of Scots.
- Because of this his house was taken from him. This could be when John Knox moved in.
- Mossman lost his life because of his support for Mary. He was hung at the Mercat Cross in 1573.
- The house gave up one of its secrets in 1990 when stone booths were uncovered on the ground floor. One of these could have been James Mossman's shop. The booths are between the ticket counter and the outside wall overlooking the High Street

Next to John Knox House was the Netherbow Port or Gate. This is where the Old Town ended. The Netherbow Port closed off the street and the arched gateway was guarded.

It must have been an impressive building, with round towers and battlements, a square clock tower and a tall pointed tower. The heads of those who'd been executed were stuck on the tops of the towers as a warning to others. The more important the person, the higher the head was put.

From the Tolbooth records: *1663 July 8th – Sir Archibold Johnston of Warriston, for treason, his head cut off and placed on the Netherbow.*

The Netherbow Port was pulled down in 1764. Brass studs on the road mark where it stood. The present Netherbow name is on a **Church of Scotland Arts Centre**. In a courtyard off the restaurant hangs the Netherbow Bell, with the words *'Council and People of Edinburgh placed me on the topmost tower. October 1621.'*

*RIGHT, DOWNHILL SIDE
OF THE HIGH STREET*

On the opposite side of the
road to John Knox House, is
the **Museum of Childhood**.
Quick Quiz 2 On the
ground floor of the museum
is a galloper. Is this
a) a wooden horse
b) an old-style bicycle?
Answer on this page
The museum has a large
collection of toy soldiers,
trains and tricycles, dolls,
books and Dinky toys.

Below the museum, **Tweeddale Court** has a
colourful entrance. The original iron gates are
painted red and gold and the name plate is also
painted gold. Inside the court is a length of
Edinburgh's oldest town wall, the **King's Wall,**
built about 1450.

The last close before St Mary's Street
is **World's End Close,** a reminder that the
Flodden Wall was here. The wall runs
through the cellars of the **World's End pub.**
There's another length, above ground, at the
foot of **St Mary's Street.**

World's End is where the Old Town of
Edinburgh did come to an end.

Quick Quiz 1 answer b) the pigs lived under
the outside stairs.
Quick Quiz 2 answer a) the galloper is a
wooden horse from an early 20th century
roundabout. His name is Alf and he's brightly
painted in red, green, gold, blue and black.

The Canongate and Holyrood

Quick Quiz 1 In Edinburgh you'll find canons and cannons. Which one would you fire?
Answer on page 46

What's in a name?

The Canongate *(the Burgh of the Canongate)* was separate from Edinburgh until 1856. It grew around **Holyrood Abbey.** The road from Holyrood was the Canon Gait, the way the canons or monks walked from the Abbey to the Netherbow Port and into Edinburgh.

In the middle of the long Canongate street was the most important building, the **Tolbooth.** It's easy to find – look for the large square Victorian clock. The Tolbooth was built in 1591 for the Canongate town council.

- The Town Council meetings were held there.
- Tolls were collected from travellers going in to Edinburgh.
- Trials were held and sentences passed.
- Prisoners were kept in the Tolbooth jail.

The Tolbooth is now a museum telling **The People's Story.** It still has a prison cell, with prisoners held inside.

RIGHT, DOWNHILL SIDE OF THE CANONGATE

Opposite the Tolbooth is **Museum of Edinburgh.**

Quick Quiz 2 The sign outside the museum is of a drummer and a town crier. Was the town crier paid a) to cry for sad people b) to cry out the news? *Answer on page 46*

HUNTLY HOUSE MUSEUM

The huge iron key to the Tolbooth is in Museum of Edinburgh. So are the collar and dinner dish belonging to Greyfriar's Bobby. There are photographs of Bobby too, sitting neatly on a chair and looking exactly like his statue near Greyfriars Church.

Lands and Closes

Many of the names in the Canongate tell you exactly who lived there or what work was done there.

- **Bakehouse Close** was once owned by the Incorporation of Bakers of the Canongate *(a trade association)*. Before that it was called Hammerman's Close.
- **Sugar House Close,** where there was a sugar refinery.
- **Chessel's Court,** built in 1745 by Archibald Chessel and now restored. This is where Deacon Brodie was discovered robbing the Excise Office (1788).

How many do you know?

'Incorporation' is the name given to trade associations in a burgh. The members shared a common craft and were skilled men.
The Canongate was the home of many trades. How many of these do you know? *(out of 7)*

Shoemakers. Hammermen. Tailors.
Weavers. Fleshers. Baxters. Barbers.

Answers. You'll know shoemakers, tailors, weavers and barbers because we use the same names today. Hammermen worked with metal, like blacksmiths and gunsmiths. Flesher was the Scots name for a butcher. Baxter was the

Scots name for a baker. The Incorporation
of Shoemakers was the oldest, with records
from 1554.

LEFT, DOWNHILL SIDE OF THE CANONGATE

185 Canongate has the name **Shoemaker's Land.**
It has a heavy carved shield over one door and
the date 1677. The crown on the shield is St
Crispin's. He's the patron saint of shoemakers.
Below the crown is a shoemaker's paring knife,
used on leather.

The Land is also known as **Bible Land**
because of the carved open book with four lines
of a psalm on it. *Behold how good a thing it is,
and how becoming well, Together such as
brethren are in unity to dwell.*

The Canongate was never as crowded as the
High Street. Many of the fine houses with their
long gardens were built for courtiers attending
the king at Holyrood. **Canongate Kirk,** with its
curving roof line, still has a very long churchyard.
It slopes away from the main street and has a
view up to **Regent Road** and the old **Royal High
School** building, in the New Town.

Do you really want to know? Buried in the
churchyard is Professor James Gregory *(died
1821)*. He invented Gregory's Powder, a mixture
of rhubarb, ginger and magnesia – a 'cure' for all
stomach upsets.

Almost next to the church is **Dunbar's Close.** Here
is one of Edinburgh's best kept secrets – a Hidden
Garden. It's laid out like a 17th century garden,
with low box hedges surrounding small garden
plots. Lavender, thyme and old fashioned roses
grow there. The old stone walls keep out the
winds. Even on cooler days there are hidden
sunny corners to sit in. *(Donated by the
Mushroom Trust in 1978. Free.)*

The poppies on the gate of **Panmure Close** are a reminder that Lady Haig's Poppy Factory was here until 1965. The red poppies are worn each November on Remembrance Sunday, remembering those who died in 20th century wars.

At the foot of the Canongate is **White Horse Close.** The White Horse Inn was here from about 1623. The Close was rebuilt nearly 350 years later, in 1965.

- There were stables here where travellers could keep their horses overnight.
- Close by was a large tank of water for the horses to drink.
- Coaches left from here for all stops to London – Berwick, Newcastle, York and further south It was a long journey, with an early morning start. A 1754 handbill outside the inn gave the details. *All that are desirous to pass from Edinburgh to London or any other place on their road, let them repair to the White Horse Cellar in Edinburgh at which place they may be received in a Stage Coach every Monday and Friday which performs the whole journey in eight days (if God permits) and sets forth at five in the morning.*

Quick Quiz 3 The White Horse was named after Mary Queen of Scots' white palfrey. Was a palfrey a) a saddle horse ridden by a woman b) a heavy-weight horse used for carrying luggage? *Answer on page 47*

In a number of places in the Canongate and Holyrood you can see a stags head, like the one in the picture. It's on the front of the Tolbooth clock, on the Canongate church and the Mercat Cross in the church grounds, and on the gates to Holyrood.

OLD TOWN TALES:
The Canongate Stag and Holyrood

At the very top of the Canongate church, above the coat of arms of William III, is the sign of the Canongate stag. It shows the head of a stag with a cross between the antlers.

The story is that King David I went hunting in the forest which then lay at the foot of the Canongate. A huge white stag charged him and knocked him from his horse. As the king lay helpless on the ground, the stag lowered his head to attack. The king thought he would be killed, and reached up to grasp the stag's antlers. Instead he found himself holding a cross which had appeared between the antlers. The stag fled.

Thankful that he was alive, King David ordered that an abbey was to be built there. It was called the Church of the Holy Rood or Cross.

This is where the name, **Holyrood,** comes from. The abbey was built long before the royal palace which is called 'the Palace of Holyroodhouse.' Most people just call it Holyrood.

The Abbey and Abbey Strand

The last short length of road in the whole of the Royal Mile is **Abbey Strand**. It begins with the brass letters **S...S...S** across the roadway. It ends at the gates of Holyrood.

OLD TOWN TALES: S...S...S

S stands for Sanctuary, a place of safety. Lords and lawyers, doctors and paupers who had got into debt were safe from arrest if they stayed here.

Nicknamed the 'Abbey Lairds', they had to live in this small part of Edinburgh or risk going to prison. Living in the Abbey Strand wasn't too bad. It had shops, inns and markets but it could get overcrowded.

Holyrood Park was also part of the Sanctuary so debtors had wide open spaces to walk in . And from midnight on Saturday to midnight on Sunday they could safely leave Abbey Strand. They could go home or visit friends, but they had to be back on Sunday night.

There are stories of Abbey Lairds walking through Holyrood Park to visit friends in Duddingston Village and not getting back in time. The answer was to stay quietly in Duddingston for a week and return the next Sunday.

Sanctuary came to an end in 1880 when the law was changed. Imprisonment for debt was ended.

When the present royal family visit Holyrood some of the court officials live in Abbey Strand.

Holyrood Abbey Fact File

The abbey was founded in 1128 by King David I.

As well as the abbey itself there were living quarters for the monks, an infirmary and a guest house.

Guests, including royal guests, enjoyed staying at the abbey. The monks brewed their own famous ale, using water from local wells and streams. Later, breweries were built here. One of the biggest breweries was very close to Holyrood palace. This is where the Scottish Parliament building is being built.

For more then 600 years the abbey was built and rebuilt. It was set on fire, attacked by a mob, and had the lead taken from the roof.

In 1758 it was given a new stone roof. The roof was so heavy that it collapsed ten years later. Holyrood Abbey has been a ruin ever since.

THE PALACE OF
HOLYROODHOUSE

The palace began as the royal guest house of the monastery. King James IV decided it should be a palace (1501). Since then it has been the scene of marriages and murders, plots and riots, funerals and fires.

- James IV, who began building the palace, was killed at the Battle of Flodden.
- Mary Queen of Scots married her 2nd and 3rd husbands at Holyrood.
- Mary's Italian secretary, David Rizzio, was stabbed to death in the palace.
- The palace was burnt by the English in 1544 and by accident in 1650.
- Oliver Cromwell's troops stayed in the palace.
- Cromwell had the Marquis of Montrose executed. When Charles II became king, the remains of the marquis were gathered up from all over Scotland. *(His head was still in Edinburgh)*. The remains lay in state in Holyrood before burial in St Giles'.
- Charles II had much of the palace rebuilt, but never visited it.
- Holyrood has been used by the royal family since the time of Queen Victoria (1837–1901).

The Palace of Holyroodhouse is open to the public daily except during Royal and State visits. Admission charge.

Quick Quiz 1 answer b) you would fire a cannon, a heavy gun mounted on a carriage. The huge **Mons Meg** in the castle is a bombard, an ancient type of cannon. It weighs 6040kg. It had the nickname 'the great iron murderer'.
Quick Quiz 2 answer a) the town crier called out the news. The beat of the drum drew

attention, then the town crier read out his news. It might be a warning that a prisoner had escaped from the Tolbooth, or the time of the next market, or even the daily price of fish.

Quick Quiz 3 answer b) a palfrey was a light-weight saddle horse usually ridden by a woman.

Ghost Tales of the Old Town

THE LOST DRUMMER BOY

It's a well-known fact that all Scottish castles have a secret passage or escape route. So Edinburgh castle must have one – but where can it be?

Many years ago the soldiers living in the castle tried to find out. They knew where an ancient and arched passageway began. None of them knew where it ended.

One quiet night they persuaded a young drummer boy to explore the passageway. 'You walk through the passage and bang on your drum,' they told him. 'We will listen and follow the sound. We'll meet you at the other end.'

So the drummer boy set off.

Beat, beat, beat, went the drum. The soldiers followed the sound. 'Keep going,' they called. 'We can hear you.'

Beat, beat, beat, went the drum. Again the soldiers followed the sound. And yet again, beat, beat, beat. And the soldiers listened and followed a winding path through the castle.

The sound grew fainter. 'Play louder,' they shouted. And for a moment the sound did grow louder, then softer, then softer still until there was nothing to hear.

The soldiers were frantic with worry. 'Play, play,' they yelled, running this way and that, listening and calling again. The castle was as silent as the grave.

The little drummer boy had vanished. He was never seen again. But he has been heard. On a quiet night, people living near the castle sometimes hear a faint sound, like the beat, beat, beat of a drum.

They say it's the little drummer boy – or his ghost – still trying to find a way out of the secret passage.

A GHOSTLY WARNING

The battle of Flodden was fought in 1513 between England and Scotland. Shortly before the battle an Edinburgh man was walking home late at night. As he got near the Mercat Cross in the High Street he heard a voice.

He looked around but could see no-one. The voice went on speaking. It came from the top of the Mercat Cross, although no-one stood there. The man stood at the foot of the Cross and listened. The voice was reading out a list of names.

On and on went the list. As the man listened, his heart almost stopped. He knew the names. They were those of his friends. Then the names of his two brothers were called out. Then his own name. He could listen no longer but rushed home, shaking and gibbering with fear.

He tried to tell his family what he had heard but they couldn't make sense of what he told them. A list of names? What list? What names? What was he gibbering about? He couldn't answer any of their questions.

Not long afterwards many Edinburgh men left the town to follow their king, James IV. He marched them to Flodden Field in Northumberland. There, on the battlefield, the king was killed. And, far from home, so were the men from Edinburgh.

All except one.

The man who had heard the ghostly list of names warning of death, was spared. He alone returned home to Edinburgh.

THE STREET OF SORROWS

The Old Town of Edinburgh has many ghostly corners but the most haunted place of all is Mary King's Close. The plague of 1645 killed most of those who lived there. The others left.

After more than a hundred years, part of the close was opened again. An elderly man and his wife moved in. They stayed for only one night. This is what happened to them.

Around midnight they were sitting by the fire. The man was reading his Bible. Slowly, the light in the room grew dim. The candle flickered and the flame turned a ghastly blue. The air grew cold.

Looking up from his reading, the man saw the head of a dead person floating in front of him. There was no body, only a head. He fainted and so did his wife. When they opened their eyes again the room was in darkness.

Then they heard a door open. Through the door came a hand holding a candle. The hand

came to where they were sitting and placed the
candle carefully on the table beside them.
Then they heard the strangest sound of all.
It was the sound of feet, skipping or dancing
across the floor.

The room felt full of ghosts, moving through
the cold air. Then, with a deep groan, they
left. The couple fled and never entered the
house again.

Nearly two hundred years later, Mary King's
Close was opened again. No-one lives there but
there are reminders of the past – a cobbled
street, fireplaces, an old mantelpiece. People
visiting the close can only guess what it was
like to live there.

*Mary King's Close is in the courtyard of the City
Chambers and there are pre-booked tours of
Edinburgh's most haunted close.*

People of The Old Town

THE TROUBLED LIFE OF MARY QUEEN OF SCOTS.
1542-1587

- Mary was born at Linlithgow Palace on 8th December 1542.
- She was the daughter of King James V of Scotland and Queen Mary.
- When she was six days old her father died. Mary became Queen of Scotland.
- She was brought up at the French court, and in 1558, at 15, married Francis, heir to the French throne.
- Over the next two years Mary's mother died in Edinburgh and Francis' father died. Francis and Mary became King and Queen of France. Then in December 1560, Francis died.

The Edinburgh Connection

On 19th August 1561, Mary returned to Scotland, landing at the port of Leith. Still in her teens, she was an orphan and a widow. She was Queen of Scots but also a stranger in her own country. She was a Catholic in a country becoming Protestant under the strong influence of John Knox.

For the next six years all the important events in her life took place in Edinburgh. She married her second husband at Holyrood. Her son, James, was born in Edinburgh Castle. Her second husband was murdered and Mary quickly married again.

The scandal of this was too great and Mary gave up the throne in 1567. Her one year old son became King James VI of Scotland.

Mary left Edinburgh. A plaque in the courtyard of the City Chambers tells of the last night she spent here. It was 15th June 1567.

From then on she was a prisoner of Queen Elizabeth of England. Elizabeth signed Mary's death warrant in February 1587 and Mary was beheaded one week later.

She was 44 years old and had been without her freedom for the last 20 of those years.

Postscript. Queen Elizabeth died in 1603. James VI of Scotland became King James I of England. It was Mary's son who united the crowns of England and Scotland.

JOHN KNOX 1514–1572.
Mary's Fiercest Foe

1. He became a Catholic priest but left the Catholic church in 1544.
2. He was captured by the French and became a galley-slave, chained, and forced to row on a French ship.
3. He led Scotland away from the Catholic faith into the Protestant faith and was the minister of St Giles' for 12 years.
4. He held strong opinions on most matters, as did the Catholic Mary Queen of Scots, so they were often in conflict.
5. He held very modern views on education for all and on helping the poor.
6. A fiery preacher, it's said that he was lifted into the pulpit to preach even when near death. He died in what is now called John Knox House.

Postscript A missing body. John Knox was buried in St Giles' churchyard, which was behind the church. It's now a car park. His grave was marked by stone number 44. The stone, with his initials and date of death, is now inside the church. It's thought that bodies from St Giles' were reburied in Greyfriars churchyard, but where is John Knox's body now? No-one can be sure.

ROBERT BURNS 1759–1796. Scotland's National Poet

Robert Burns was born into an Ayrshire farming family. His farming life was not very successful and he thought of emigrating to Jamaica. When his first book of poetry was an immediate success he stayed in Scotland.

His poems were published by the Edinburgh bookseller, William Creech, who had a bookshop in the Luckenbooths, tiny shops beside St Giles'. When Burns visited William Creech, he stayed in the Lawnmarket and the Grassmarket, in the Old Town.

Burns' birthday, on 25th January, is celebrated by Scots all over the world, often with a Burns Supper of haggis and neeps, with whisky to drink.

In 1985 a huge stained glass window in honour of Robert Burns was installed in St Giles'. It was designed by an Icelandic artist, Leifur Breidfjord.

Robert Burns wrote: *Should auld acquaintance be forgot, And never brought to mind? We'll tak a cup o' kindness yet, For auld lang syne.*

SIR WALTER SCOTT 1771–1832.
The Hardest Working Writer

Walter Scott was born in Edinburgh's Old Town, went to the High School (where Bailie Macmorran had been killed), and to Edinburgh University. From childhood he was lame in his right foot and walked with a limp.

For the last 30 years of his life he never stopped writing. His printer and his publisher went bankrupt and Scott hastened his own death through debts and overwork.

He was in Edinburgh when the old Tolbooth was pulled down and took the wooden door for his country house, Abbotsford, in the Scottish Borders. He also saw the Great Fire of 1824.

His huge memorial is the **Scott Monument** in East Princes Street Gardens. It has a circular stair and 287 steps to the top.

Walter Scott wrote: *O what a tangled web we weave, When first we practise to deceive.*

ROBERT LOUIS STEVENSON
1850–1894. Far From Home

Robert Louis Stevenson was born in the New Town and studied law at Edinburgh University. He was described as being very thin with dark, shining eyes. His health was often poor and Edinburgh's strong north winds and cold sea mists made it worse.

For the last five years of his life he lived in Samoa, in the South Seas. He died there, of tuberculosis, and was buried on a mountain top. Even living so far away, he never lost his love of Scotland. Many of his poems are a happy remembrance of his Edinburgh childhood. His books, especially *Treasure*

Island, are full of adventure and excitement.

There's a memorial to him on one wall in St Giles'. It's said that the Stevenson family didn't like it. It shows the writer as an invalid, resting with a rug over his knees.

Robert Louis Stevenson wrote: *Fifteen men on the dead man's chest – Yo-ho-ho and a bottle of rum! Drink and the devil had done for the rest.*

Words, Words, Words.

EXTINCT	not active.
FRANTIC	mad with fear.
GAELIC	the Celtic language of the Scots.
GIBBERING	to talk quickly, not making sense.
HAGGIS & NEEPS	haggis is a Scottish dish made from offal, oatmeal, suet and seasonings. Neeps are turnips.
JUNCTION	where roads meet or cross.
KIRK	Scots name for a church, usually Church of Scotland.
LOCH	Scots name for a lake or pond.
MAKAR	in Makar's Court, this means a craftsman or woman whose skill is writing.
MINISTER	a clergyman, especially of the Church of Scotland.
PORTCULLIS	a castle or town gate which can be lowered to keep attackers out.
SMOTHER	to suffocate; to cut off the air needed to breathe.
TENEMENT	a tall building divided into rooms or flats.

Twenty Questions

1. If you heard the call 'Gardyloo' what would you do?
2. Where would you see diamond-patterned legs?
3. There are two statues on Edinburgh Castle gatehouse. One is King Robert the Bruce. Who is the other statue of?
4. Where is the tallest spire in the Old Town?
5. Where will you find four dragons?
6. Who lived a double life?
7. The keys to the city are tied with black and white ribbon. How many keys are there?
8. You won't find horses in King's Stables Road now. What will you find?
9. What is above the entrance to Old Fishmarket Close?
10. What did people in the Old Town use before there were taxis?
11. Which statue became bandy-legged?
12. What animal did Lord Gardenstone allow to sleep in his bed?
13. What happened to Sir Archibold Johnston's head?
14. What did Professor James Gregory invent, and would you like it?
15. Name one place where you can see the Canongate stag.
16. Who or what was Mons Meg?
17. Who got lost in Edinburgh Castle?
18. What is the name of Edinburgh's most haunted close?
19. Whose body has gone missing? *(He was an important man)*
20. Whose birthday is celebrated with a meal of haggis, neeps and whisky?

Answers to Twenty Questions

1. Run for cover before you got soaked.
2. At the Festival Fringe Society, 180 High Street.
3. William Wallace.
4. On The Hub, Castlehill.
5. Wardrop's Court, Lawnmarket.
6. Deacon William Brodie.
7. Two keys.
8. A multi-storey car park.
9. A line of swimming fish.
10. They used sedan chairs.
11. The statue of Charles II in Parliament Square.
12. His pet pig.
13. It was stuck on a tower of the Netherbow Port.
14. He invented Gregory's Powder for stomach upsets. It was a mixture of rhubarb, ginger and magnesia. Would you like it?
15. On the Tolbooth Clock. On the top of Canongate Kirk and on the Mercat Cross. On the gates to Holyrood Palace.
16. A huge heavy cannon, now in Edinburgh Castle.
17. A little drummer boy.
18. Mary King's Close.
19. John Knox, minister of St Giles'.
20. Robert Burns, Scotland's national poet.

MILTON COLLEGE LIBRARY